50 Roasting Food for Home Recipes

By: Kelly Johnson

Table of Contents

- Roasted Chicken with Garlic and Herbs
- Roasted Sweet Potatoes
- Roasted Brussels Sprouts
- Garlic Roasted Carrots
- Herb-Crusted Roast Beef
- Roasted Cauliflower with Parmesan
- Roasted Potatoes with Rosemary
- Roasted Salmon with Lemon and Dill
- Roasted Asparagus with Balsamic Glaze
- Roasted Butternut Squash
- Roasted Zucchini with Parmesan
- Roasted Beets with Thyme
- Roasted Eggplant with Olive Oil
- Roasted Mushrooms with Garlic and Thyme
- Honey Roasted Parsnips
- Roasted Bell Peppers
- Roasted Brussels Sprouts with Bacon
- Roasted Fennel with Lemon
- Roasted Pork Loin with Apples
- Roasted Cherry Tomatoes
- Roasted Spaghetti Squash
- Roasted Chicken Thighs with Paprika
- Roasted Broccoli with Lemon
- Roasted Lamb with Rosemary and Garlic
- Roasted Red Potatoes with Dill
- Roasted Green Beans with Almonds
- Roasted Garlic and Herb Shrimp
- Roasted Radishes with Butter
- Roasted Peppers and Onions
- Roasted Corn on the Cob
- Roasted Brussel Sprouts with Cranberries
- Roasted Acorn Squash
- Roasted Sweet Potatoes with Cinnamon
- Roasted Vegetables Medley
- Roasted Balsamic Chicken

- Roasted Carrot and Beet Salad
- Roasted Figs with Honey
- Roasted Artichokes with Garlic
- Roasted Potatoes with Mustard Seeds
- Roasted Pomegranate Chicken
- Roasted Plantains
- Roasted Garlic and Parmesan Broccoli
- Roasted Cauliflower Rice
- Roasted Pork Belly with Crackling
- Roasted Pineapple with Brown Sugar
- Roasted Spiced Chickpeas
- Roasted Salmon with Honey Mustard Glaze
- Roasted Bell Peppers Stuffed with Rice
- Roasted Tomato Soup
- Roasted Chicken with Lemons and Olives

Roasted Chicken with Garlic and Herbs

Ingredients:

- 1 whole chicken (about 4 lbs)
- 6 garlic cloves, minced
- 2 tbsp fresh rosemary, chopped
- 2 tbsp fresh thyme, chopped
- 1 lemon, halved
- 2 tbsp olive oil
- Salt and pepper to taste

Instructions:

1. Preheat oven to 425°F (220°C).
2. In a small bowl, mix minced garlic, rosemary, thyme, olive oil, salt, and pepper.
3. Rub the chicken inside and out with the garlic and herb mixture.
4. Stuff the chicken cavity with lemon halves.
5. Place the chicken on a roasting rack in a baking pan.
6. Roast for 1 hour 15 minutes to 1 hour 30 minutes, or until the internal temperature reaches 165°F (75°C).
7. Let the chicken rest for 10 minutes before carving.

Roasted Sweet Potatoes

Ingredients:

- 4 medium sweet potatoes, peeled and cubed
- 2 tbsp olive oil
- 1 tsp ground cinnamon
- 1/2 tsp ground nutmeg
- Salt and pepper to taste

Instructions:

1. Preheat oven to 400°F (200°C).
2. Toss the cubed sweet potatoes with olive oil, cinnamon, nutmeg, salt, and pepper.
3. Spread the sweet potatoes in a single layer on a baking sheet.
4. Roast for 25-30 minutes, flipping halfway through, until tender and slightly caramelized.

Roasted Brussels Sprouts

Ingredients:

- 1 lb Brussels sprouts, trimmed and halved
- 2 tbsp olive oil
- Salt and pepper to taste
- 1 tbsp balsamic vinegar (optional)

Instructions:

1. Preheat oven to 400°F (200°C).
2. Toss Brussels sprouts with olive oil, salt, and pepper.
3. Spread them out on a baking sheet in a single layer.
4. Roast for 20-25 minutes, shaking the pan halfway through.
5. Drizzle with balsamic vinegar just before serving (optional).

Garlic Roasted Carrots

Ingredients:

- 1 lb carrots, peeled and cut into sticks
- 3 garlic cloves, minced
- 2 tbsp olive oil
- 1 tsp dried thyme
- Salt and pepper to taste

Instructions:

1. Preheat oven to 425°F (220°C).
2. Toss the carrots with garlic, olive oil, thyme, salt, and pepper.
3. Spread them out on a baking sheet in a single layer.
4. Roast for 25-30 minutes, or until tender and caramelized, flipping halfway through.

Herb-Crusted Roast Beef

Ingredients:

- 3 lb beef roast (such as ribeye or sirloin)
- 3 tbsp olive oil
- 4 garlic cloves, minced
- 2 tbsp fresh rosemary, chopped
- 2 tbsp fresh thyme, chopped
- Salt and pepper to taste

Instructions:

1. Preheat oven to 450°F (230°C).
2. Rub the beef roast with olive oil, garlic, rosemary, thyme, salt, and pepper.
3. Place the roast on a rack in a roasting pan.
4. Roast for 15 minutes, then reduce the temperature to 350°F (175°C).
5. Continue roasting for 1-1.5 hours, or until the internal temperature reaches 135°F (57°C) for medium-rare.
6. Let rest for 10 minutes before slicing.

Roasted Cauliflower with Parmesan

Ingredients:

- 1 head cauliflower, cut into florets
- 2 tbsp olive oil
- 1/2 cup grated Parmesan cheese
- Salt and pepper to taste
- 1 tbsp fresh parsley, chopped (optional)

Instructions:

1. Preheat oven to 400°F (200°C).
2. Toss cauliflower florets with olive oil, salt, and pepper.
3. Spread them on a baking sheet in a single layer.
4. Roast for 25-30 minutes, until tender and golden.
5. Sprinkle with Parmesan cheese and roast for an additional 5 minutes.
6. Garnish with fresh parsley if desired.

Roasted Potatoes with Rosemary

Ingredients:

- 1.5 lbs baby potatoes, halved
- 2 tbsp olive oil
- 1 tbsp fresh rosemary, chopped
- Salt and pepper to taste

Instructions:

1. Preheat oven to 425°F (220°C).
2. Toss the potatoes with olive oil, rosemary, salt, and pepper.
3. Spread them out on a baking sheet in a single layer.
4. Roast for 25-30 minutes, flipping halfway through, until crispy and golden.

Roasted Salmon with Lemon and Dill

Ingredients:

- 4 salmon fillets
- 1 lemon, thinly sliced
- 2 tbsp fresh dill, chopped
- 1 tbsp olive oil
- Salt and pepper to taste

Instructions:

1. Preheat oven to 375°F (190°C).
2. Place salmon fillets on a baking sheet lined with parchment paper.
3. Drizzle with olive oil, and season with salt and pepper.
4. Top with lemon slices and dill.
5. Roast for 12-15 minutes, or until the salmon is cooked through.

Roasted Asparagus with Balsamic Glaze

Ingredients:

- 1 lb asparagus, trimmed
- 2 tbsp olive oil
- Salt and pepper to taste
- 1 tbsp balsamic vinegar

Instructions:

1. Preheat oven to 425°F (220°C).
2. Toss asparagus with olive oil, salt, and pepper.
3. Spread the asparagus on a baking sheet in a single layer.
4. Roast for 12-15 minutes, or until tender.
5. Drizzle with balsamic vinegar before serving.

Roasted Butternut Squash

Ingredients:

- 1 medium butternut squash, peeled and cubed
- 2 tbsp olive oil
- 1 tsp ground cinnamon
- Salt and pepper to taste
- 1 tbsp maple syrup (optional)

Instructions:

1. Preheat oven to 400°F (200°C).
2. Toss the butternut squash cubes with olive oil, cinnamon, salt, and pepper.
3. Spread them on a baking sheet in a single layer.
4. Roast for 25-30 minutes, turning halfway through, until tender.
5. If desired, drizzle with maple syrup before serving.

Roasted Zucchini with Parmesan

Ingredients:

- 4 medium zucchinis, sliced into rounds
- 2 tbsp olive oil
- 1/4 cup grated Parmesan cheese
- 1/2 tsp garlic powder
- Salt and pepper to taste

Instructions:

1. Preheat oven to 425°F (220°C).
2. Toss zucchini slices with olive oil, garlic powder, salt, and pepper.
3. Arrange the zucchini on a baking sheet in a single layer.
4. Sprinkle with Parmesan cheese.
5. Roast for 20-25 minutes, until golden and tender.

Roasted Beets with Thyme

Ingredients:

- 4 medium beets, peeled and cubed
- 2 tbsp olive oil
- 2 sprigs fresh thyme
- Salt and pepper to taste

Instructions:

1. Preheat oven to 400°F (200°C).
2. Toss beets with olive oil, salt, and pepper.
3. Place beets on a baking sheet, and scatter thyme sprigs over them.
4. Roast for 35-40 minutes, flipping halfway through, until tender.

Roasted Eggplant with Olive Oil

Ingredients:

- 2 medium eggplants, sliced into 1-inch rounds
- 3 tbsp olive oil
- Salt and pepper to taste
- 1/2 tsp dried oregano (optional)

Instructions:

1. Preheat oven to 400°F (200°C).
2. Brush eggplant slices with olive oil and season with salt, pepper, and oregano.
3. Arrange on a baking sheet in a single layer.
4. Roast for 25-30 minutes, flipping halfway through, until golden and tender.

Roasted Mushrooms with Garlic and Thyme

Ingredients:

- 1 lb mushrooms, cleaned and halved
- 2 tbsp olive oil
- 3 garlic cloves, minced
- 2 sprigs fresh thyme
- Salt and pepper to taste

Instructions:

1. Preheat oven to 400°F (200°C).
2. Toss mushrooms with olive oil, garlic, thyme, salt, and pepper.
3. Spread them out on a baking sheet.
4. Roast for 20-25 minutes, stirring halfway through, until tender and golden.

Honey Roasted Parsnips

Ingredients:

- 4 medium parsnips, peeled and cut into sticks
- 2 tbsp olive oil
- 1 tbsp honey
- Salt and pepper to taste

Instructions:

1. Preheat oven to 400°F (200°C).
2. Toss parsnips with olive oil, honey, salt, and pepper.
3. Spread them out on a baking sheet in a single layer.
4. Roast for 25-30 minutes, flipping halfway through, until tender and caramelized.

Roasted Bell Peppers

Ingredients:

- 4 bell peppers (any color), halved and seeded
- 2 tbsp olive oil
- 1 tsp smoked paprika (optional)
- Salt and pepper to taste

Instructions:

1. Preheat oven to 425°F (220°C).
2. Toss bell pepper halves with olive oil, smoked paprika, salt, and pepper.
3. Arrange on a baking sheet, cut side down.
4. Roast for 20-25 minutes, until the skins are charred and the peppers are soft.
5. Optional: Peel the skins after roasting for a smoother texture.

Roasted Brussels Sprouts with Bacon

Ingredients:

- 1 lb Brussels sprouts, trimmed and halved
- 2 tbsp olive oil
- 4 slices bacon, chopped
- Salt and pepper to taste

Instructions:

1. Preheat oven to 400°F (200°C).
2. Toss Brussels sprouts with olive oil, salt, and pepper.
3. Spread Brussels sprouts on a baking sheet.
4. Scatter chopped bacon over the Brussels sprouts.
5. Roast for 25-30 minutes, stirring halfway through, until crispy and caramelized.

Roasted Fennel with Lemon

Ingredients:

- 2 fennel bulbs, trimmed and sliced into wedges
- 2 tbsp olive oil
- 1 lemon, sliced into rounds
- Salt and pepper to taste
- 1 tbsp fresh parsley, chopped (optional)

Instructions:

1. Preheat oven to 400°F (200°C).
2. Toss fennel wedges with olive oil, salt, and pepper.
3. Arrange fennel on a baking sheet and top with lemon slices.
4. Roast for 25-30 minutes, until tender and slightly caramelized.
5. Garnish with fresh parsley before serving if desired.

Roasted Pork Loin with Apples

Ingredients:

- 1.5 lbs pork loin
- 2 tbsp olive oil
- 2 apples, cored and sliced
- 1 onion, sliced
- 1 tsp dried thyme
- Salt and pepper to taste
- 1/2 cup chicken broth
- 2 tbsp honey (optional)

Instructions:

1. Preheat oven to 400°F (200°C).
2. Season the pork loin with olive oil, thyme, salt, and pepper.
3. Arrange apple and onion slices in the bottom of a roasting pan.
4. Place the pork loin on top of the apples and onions.
5. Pour chicken broth into the pan and drizzle the pork with honey if desired.
6. Roast for 30-35 minutes, until the pork reaches an internal temperature of 145°F (63°C).
7. Let the pork rest for 5 minutes before slicing and serving with the roasted apples and onions.

Roasted Cherry Tomatoes

Ingredients:

- 2 cups cherry tomatoes, halved
- 2 tbsp olive oil
- 2 garlic cloves, minced
- Salt and pepper to taste
- 1 tsp balsamic vinegar (optional)
- Fresh basil, chopped (optional)

Instructions:

1. Preheat oven to 375°F (190°C).
2. Toss halved cherry tomatoes with olive oil, garlic, salt, and pepper.
3. Spread them out in a single layer on a baking sheet.
4. Roast for 20-25 minutes, until the tomatoes are soft and slightly caramelized.
5. Drizzle with balsamic vinegar and sprinkle with fresh basil before serving, if desired.

Roasted Spaghetti Squash

Ingredients:

- 1 medium spaghetti squash
- 2 tbsp olive oil
- Salt and pepper to taste
- 1/2 tsp garlic powder (optional)

Instructions:

1. Preheat oven to 400°F (200°C).
2. Slice the spaghetti squash in half lengthwise and remove the seeds.
3. Drizzle the flesh with olive oil, salt, pepper, and garlic powder.
4. Place the squash halves cut side down on a baking sheet.
5. Roast for 30-40 minutes, until the flesh is tender and easily shredded with a fork.
6. Use a fork to scrape the flesh into spaghetti-like strands and serve.

Roasted Chicken Thighs with Paprika

Ingredients:

- 6 bone-in, skin-on chicken thighs
- 2 tbsp olive oil
- 1 tsp paprika
- 1/2 tsp garlic powder
- Salt and pepper to taste
- Fresh parsley for garnish (optional)

Instructions:

1. Preheat oven to 425°F (220°C).
2. Toss chicken thighs with olive oil, paprika, garlic powder, salt, and pepper.
3. Arrange the thighs on a baking sheet, skin side up.
4. Roast for 35-40 minutes, until the chicken is crispy and cooked through (internal temperature of 165°F or 74°C).
5. Garnish with fresh parsley before serving, if desired.

Roasted Broccoli with Lemon

Ingredients:

- 1 lb broccoli florets
- 2 tbsp olive oil
- 1 lemon, sliced
- 1/2 tsp garlic powder
- Salt and pepper to taste
- Fresh Parmesan (optional)

Instructions:

1. Preheat oven to 400°F (200°C).
2. Toss broccoli florets with olive oil, garlic powder, salt, and pepper.
3. Arrange on a baking sheet and scatter lemon slices over the broccoli.
4. Roast for 20-25 minutes, until the broccoli is tender and slightly crispy.
5. Sprinkle with fresh Parmesan before serving, if desired.

Roasted Lamb with Rosemary and Garlic

Ingredients:

- 2 lbs lamb leg, bone-in or boneless
- 3 garlic cloves, minced
- 2 tbsp fresh rosemary, chopped
- 2 tbsp olive oil
- Salt and pepper to taste

Instructions:

1. Preheat oven to 400°F (200°C).
2. Rub lamb with olive oil, garlic, rosemary, salt, and pepper.
3. Place the lamb in a roasting pan.
4. Roast for 45-50 minutes, until the lamb reaches your desired doneness (medium-rare: 135°F or 57°C).
5. Let the lamb rest for 10 minutes before slicing and serving.

Roasted Red Potatoes with Dill

Ingredients:

- 1 lb red potatoes, quartered
- 2 tbsp olive oil
- 1 tsp dried dill
- Salt and pepper to taste

Instructions:

1. Preheat oven to 425°F (220°C).
2. Toss potato wedges with olive oil, dill, salt, and pepper.
3. Spread the potatoes in a single layer on a baking sheet.
4. Roast for 30-35 minutes, flipping halfway through, until golden and crispy on the edges.

Roasted Green Beans with Almonds

Ingredients:

- 1 lb green beans, trimmed
- 2 tbsp olive oil
- 1/2 cup sliced almonds
- Salt and pepper to taste

Instructions:

1. Preheat oven to 400°F (200°C).
2. Toss green beans with olive oil, salt, and pepper.
3. Spread them on a baking sheet in a single layer.
4. Roast for 20-25 minutes, until tender.
5. In the last 5 minutes of roasting, add the sliced almonds and continue roasting until golden.

Roasted Garlic and Herb Shrimp

Ingredients:

- 1 lb large shrimp, peeled and deveined
- 3 tbsp olive oil
- 4 garlic cloves, minced
- 1 tbsp fresh parsley, chopped
- 1 tsp fresh lemon juice
- Salt and pepper to taste

Instructions:

1. Preheat oven to 400°F (200°C).
2. Toss shrimp with olive oil, garlic, parsley, lemon juice, salt, and pepper.
3. Spread shrimp out on a baking sheet.
4. Roast for 8-10 minutes, until shrimp are pink and opaque.

Roasted Radishes with Butter

Ingredients:

- 1 lb radishes, trimmed and halved
- 2 tbsp butter, melted
- 1 tbsp olive oil
- Salt and pepper to taste
- Fresh parsley, chopped (optional)

Instructions:

1. Preheat oven to 400°F (200°C).
2. Toss radishes with melted butter, olive oil, salt, and pepper.
3. Spread them out on a baking sheet in a single layer.
4. Roast for 20-25 minutes, until tender and slightly caramelized.
5. Garnish with fresh parsley before serving, if desired.

Roasted Peppers and Onions

Ingredients:

- 2 bell peppers, sliced
- 1 large onion, sliced
- 2 tbsp olive oil
- 1 tsp dried oregano
- Salt and pepper to taste

Instructions:

1. Preheat oven to 425°F (220°C).
2. Toss peppers and onions with olive oil, oregano, salt, and pepper.
3. Spread them on a baking sheet in a single layer.
4. Roast for 20-25 minutes, stirring halfway through, until the vegetables are tender and slightly charred.

Roasted Corn on the Cob

Ingredients:

- 4 ears of corn, husked
- 2 tbsp olive oil or butter
- Salt and pepper to taste

Instructions:

1. Preheat oven to 400°F (200°C).
2. Rub the corn with olive oil or butter, and season with salt and pepper.
3. Wrap each ear of corn in foil and place on a baking sheet.
4. Roast for 25-30 minutes, turning halfway through.
5. Serve with additional butter and seasoning if desired.

Roasted Acorn Squash

Ingredients:

- 1 acorn squash, halved and seeded
- 2 tbsp olive oil
- 1 tbsp brown sugar
- Salt and pepper to taste
- Cinnamon (optional)

Instructions:

1. Preheat oven to 400°F (200°C).
2. Brush the inside of the squash halves with olive oil, sprinkle with brown sugar, salt, and pepper.
3. Place the squash halves cut-side down on a baking sheet.
4. Roast for 35-40 minutes, until the squash is tender.
5. Sprinkle with cinnamon if desired before serving.

Roasted Sweet Potatoes with Cinnamon

Ingredients:

- 2 large sweet potatoes, peeled and cut into cubes
- 2 tbsp olive oil
- 1 tsp ground cinnamon
- Salt to taste

Instructions:

1. Preheat oven to 400°F (200°C).
2. Toss sweet potato cubes with olive oil, cinnamon, and salt.
3. Spread them out on a baking sheet in a single layer.
4. Roast for 25-30 minutes, turning halfway, until golden and tender.

Roasted Vegetables Medley

Ingredients:

- 1 cup carrots, sliced
- 1 cup bell peppers, chopped
- 1 cup zucchini, sliced
- 1 cup red onions, sliced
- 2 tbsp olive oil
- 1 tsp dried thyme
- Salt and pepper to taste

Instructions:

1. Preheat oven to 425°F (220°C).
2. Toss vegetables with olive oil, thyme, salt, and pepper.
3. Spread them out on a baking sheet in a single layer.
4. Roast for 25-30 minutes, stirring halfway, until vegetables are tender and lightly browned.

Roasted Balsamic Chicken

Ingredients:

- 4 chicken thighs or breasts
- 1/4 cup balsamic vinegar
- 2 tbsp olive oil
- 1 tsp dried rosemary
- Salt and pepper to taste

Instructions:

1. Preheat oven to 425°F (220°C).
2. Mix balsamic vinegar, olive oil, rosemary, salt, and pepper in a bowl.
3. Coat the chicken with the balsamic mixture.
4. Place the chicken on a baking sheet and roast for 30-35 minutes, until the chicken is cooked through (internal temperature of 165°F or 74°C).

Roasted Carrot and Beet Salad

Ingredients:

- 2 cups baby carrots
- 2 medium beets, peeled and sliced
- 2 tbsp olive oil
- 1 tbsp balsamic vinegar
- Salt and pepper to taste
- Fresh arugula or spinach (optional)

Instructions:

1. Preheat oven to 400°F (200°C).
2. Toss carrots and beets with olive oil, balsamic vinegar, salt, and pepper.
3. Spread on a baking sheet in a single layer.
4. Roast for 30-35 minutes, until the vegetables are tender.
5. Serve on a bed of arugula or spinach if desired.

Roasted Figs with Honey

Ingredients:

- 8 fresh figs, halved
- 2 tbsp honey
- 1 tbsp olive oil
- Fresh thyme (optional)

Instructions:

1. Preheat oven to 375°F (190°C).
2. Arrange fig halves on a baking sheet, drizzle with honey and olive oil.
3. Roast for 15-20 minutes, until figs are softened and slightly caramelized.
4. Garnish with fresh thyme before serving if desired.

Roasted Artichokes with Garlic

Ingredients:

- 4 artichokes, trimmed and halved
- 4 cloves garlic, minced
- 2 tbsp olive oil
- 1 tbsp lemon juice
- Salt and pepper to taste
- Fresh parsley for garnish (optional)

Instructions:

1. Preheat the oven to 400°F (200°C).
2. Rub the cut sides of the artichokes with lemon juice to prevent browning.
3. Toss the artichokes with olive oil, garlic, salt, and pepper.
4. Arrange the artichokes cut-side down on a baking sheet.
5. Roast for 35-40 minutes, until the artichokes are tender.
6. Garnish with fresh parsley before serving, if desired.

Roasted Potatoes with Mustard Seeds

Ingredients:

- 1 lb baby potatoes, halved
- 2 tbsp olive oil
- 1 tbsp mustard seeds
- 1 tsp ground turmeric
- Salt and pepper to taste
- Fresh cilantro for garnish (optional)

Instructions:

1. Preheat the oven to 425°F (220°C).
2. In a small pan, heat olive oil over medium heat. Add mustard seeds and cook for 1-2 minutes until they start popping.
3. Toss the potatoes with the mustard seed oil, turmeric, salt, and pepper.
4. Spread the potatoes in a single layer on a baking sheet.
5. Roast for 25-30 minutes, turning halfway through, until the potatoes are golden and crispy.
6. Garnish with fresh cilantro before serving, if desired.

Roasted Pomegranate Chicken

Ingredients:

- 4 chicken thighs or breasts
- 1/2 cup pomegranate seeds
- 1/4 cup pomegranate molasses
- 2 tbsp olive oil
- 1 tbsp fresh thyme, chopped
- Salt and pepper to taste

Instructions:

1. Preheat the oven to 400°F (200°C).
2. In a bowl, mix the pomegranate molasses, olive oil, thyme, salt, and pepper.
3. Coat the chicken with the pomegranate mixture and place it on a baking sheet.
4. Roast for 30-35 minutes, until the chicken is cooked through (internal temperature of 165°F or 74°C).
5. Sprinkle pomegranate seeds over the chicken before serving for a fresh, fruity finish.

Roasted Plantains

Ingredients:

- 2 ripe plantains, peeled and sliced
- 2 tbsp olive oil
- 1 tsp ground cinnamon
- 1 tbsp honey (optional)
- Salt to taste

Instructions:

1. Preheat the oven to 400°F (200°C).
2. Toss the plantain slices with olive oil, cinnamon, salt, and honey (if using).
3. Arrange the slices in a single layer on a baking sheet.
4. Roast for 20-25 minutes, flipping halfway through, until the plantains are golden and slightly caramelized.

Roasted Garlic and Parmesan Broccoli

Ingredients:

- 2 heads of broccoli, cut into florets
- 4 cloves garlic, minced
- 2 tbsp olive oil
- 1/4 cup grated Parmesan cheese
- Salt and pepper to taste
- Lemon wedges for serving (optional)

Instructions:

1. Preheat the oven to 425°F (220°C).
2. Toss broccoli florets with olive oil, garlic, salt, and pepper.
3. Spread the broccoli out on a baking sheet.
4. Roast for 20-25 minutes, until tender and slightly crispy.
5. Sprinkle grated Parmesan cheese over the broccoli during the last 5 minutes of roasting.
6. Serve with a squeeze of lemon juice, if desired.

Roasted Cauliflower Rice

Ingredients:

- 1 head of cauliflower, cut into florets
- 2 tbsp olive oil
- 1/2 tsp garlic powder
- Salt and pepper to taste
- Fresh parsley for garnish (optional)

Instructions:

1. Preheat the oven to 400°F (200°C).
2. Pulse cauliflower florets in a food processor until they resemble rice grains.
3. Toss the cauliflower rice with olive oil, garlic powder, salt, and pepper.
4. Spread it out in an even layer on a baking sheet.
5. Roast for 15-20 minutes, stirring halfway through, until the cauliflower is tender and slightly browned.
6. Garnish with fresh parsley before serving, if desired.

Roasted Pork Belly with Crackling

Ingredients:

- 2 lb pork belly, skin scored
- 1 tbsp olive oil
- 1 tbsp sea salt
- 1 tsp black pepper
- 1 tsp dried rosemary
- 1/2 tsp garlic powder

Instructions:

1. Preheat the oven to 450°F (230°C).
2. Rub the pork belly with olive oil, sea salt, pepper, rosemary, and garlic powder.
3. Place the pork belly on a roasting rack in a baking tray, skin side up.
4. Roast for 20-25 minutes, until the skin starts to crisp up.
5. Lower the oven temperature to 350°F (175°C) and roast for another 1.5 hours, until the pork is tender and the skin is crispy.
6. Let the pork rest for 10 minutes before slicing and serving.

Roasted Pineapple with Brown Sugar

Ingredients:

- 1 ripe pineapple, peeled and cut into rings or wedges
- 1/4 cup brown sugar
- 1/2 tsp ground cinnamon
- 1 tbsp butter, melted
- A pinch of salt

Instructions:

1. Preheat the oven to 400°F (200°C).
2. Arrange the pineapple slices on a baking sheet.
3. In a small bowl, mix the brown sugar, cinnamon, melted butter, and a pinch of salt.
4. Drizzle the mixture over the pineapple.
5. Roast for 15-20 minutes, flipping the pineapple halfway through, until golden and caramelized.
6. Serve warm for a sweet treat.

Roasted Spiced Chickpeas

Ingredients:

- 1 can (15 oz) chickpeas, drained and rinsed
- 1 tbsp olive oil
- 1 tsp ground cumin
- 1/2 tsp paprika
- 1/2 tsp garlic powder
- Salt and pepper to taste
- 1 tbsp lemon juice (optional)

Instructions:

1. Preheat the oven to 400°F (200°C).
2. Pat the chickpeas dry with a paper towel and toss them in olive oil.
3. Mix in cumin, paprika, garlic powder, salt, and pepper.
4. Spread the chickpeas out on a baking sheet in a single layer.
5. Roast for 20-25 minutes, shaking the pan halfway through, until crispy and golden.
6. Drizzle with lemon juice before serving, if desired.

Roasted Salmon with Honey Mustard Glaze

Ingredients:

- 4 salmon fillets
- 2 tbsp Dijon mustard
- 2 tbsp honey
- 1 tbsp olive oil
- 1 tbsp lemon juice
- Salt and pepper to taste

Instructions:

1. Preheat the oven to 400°F (200°C).
2. In a small bowl, whisk together Dijon mustard, honey, olive oil, lemon juice, salt, and pepper.
3. Place the salmon fillets on a baking sheet lined with parchment paper.
4. Brush the honey mustard glaze generously over the salmon.
5. Roast for 12-15 minutes, until the salmon is cooked through and flakes easily with a fork.
6. Serve with your favorite side dishes.

Roasted Bell Peppers Stuffed with Rice

Ingredients:

- 4 bell peppers, tops cut off and seeds removed
- 1 cup cooked rice (white or brown)
- 1/2 cup grated cheese (cheddar or mozzarella)
- 1/4 cup chopped fresh parsley
- 1/2 tsp ground cumin
- 1/4 tsp chili flakes (optional)
- Salt and pepper to taste

Instructions:

1. Preheat the oven to 375°F (190°C).
2. In a bowl, combine the cooked rice, cheese, parsley, cumin, chili flakes (if using), salt, and pepper.
3. Stuff the bell peppers with the rice mixture.
4. Place the stuffed peppers on a baking dish.
5. Roast for 25-30 minutes, until the peppers are tender and the cheese is melted.
6. Serve warm, garnished with extra parsley if desired.

Roasted Tomato Soup

Ingredients:

- 4 large tomatoes, halved
- 1 onion, quartered
- 4 cloves garlic, peeled
- 1 tbsp olive oil
- Salt and pepper to taste
- 2 cups vegetable or chicken broth
- 1/4 cup heavy cream (optional)
- Fresh basil for garnish (optional)

Instructions:

1. Preheat the oven to 400°F (200°C).
2. Place the tomatoes, onion, and garlic on a baking sheet. Drizzle with olive oil and sprinkle with salt and pepper.
3. Roast for 20-25 minutes, until the vegetables are soft and slightly caramelized.
4. Transfer the roasted vegetables to a blender or food processor and blend until smooth.
5. Pour the blended soup into a pot and add the broth. Bring to a simmer over medium heat.
6. Stir in heavy cream, if using, and adjust seasoning with salt and pepper.
7. Serve warm, garnished with fresh basil if desired.

Roasted Chicken with Lemons and Olives

Ingredients:

- 1 whole chicken (about 4 lbs)
- 2 lemons, quartered
- 1 cup green olives, pitted
- 3 cloves garlic, smashed
- 2 tbsp olive oil
- 1 tbsp fresh rosemary, chopped
- Salt and pepper to taste

Instructions:

1. Preheat the oven to 425°F (220°C).
2. Rub the chicken with olive oil, rosemary, salt, and pepper.
3. Stuff the cavity of the chicken with lemon quarters, garlic, and olives.
4. Place the chicken on a roasting pan, and arrange any leftover lemon, garlic, and olives around the chicken.
5. Roast for 1 to 1.5 hours, until the chicken is golden and the internal temperature reaches 165°F (74°C).
6. Let the chicken rest for 10 minutes before carving. Serve with the roasted lemon and olives.

Roasted Brussels Sprouts with Cranberries

Ingredients:

- 1 lb Brussels sprouts, trimmed and halved
- 1/2 cup dried cranberries
- 2 tbsp olive oil
- 1 tbsp balsamic vinegar
- Salt and pepper to taste

Instructions:

1. Preheat the oven to 400°F (200°C).
2. Toss the Brussels sprouts with olive oil, balsamic vinegar, salt, and pepper.
3. Spread the Brussels sprouts on a baking sheet in a single layer.
4. Roast for 20-25 minutes, until crispy and golden.
5. Add the dried cranberries during the last 5 minutes of roasting.
6. Serve warm as a flavorful side dish.

www.ingramcontent.com/pod-product-compliance
Lightning Source LLC
LaVergne TN
LVHW081502060526
838201LV00056BA/2888